The Boomer's Guide to *Lightweight* Backpacking

Carol Corbridge

Artwork by Jayna Harrison

The Boomer's Guide to *Lightweight* Backpacking

Carol Corbridge

Artwork by Jayna Harrison

Frank Amato PUBLICATIONS, INC.

About the Author

Carol started her backpacking career as a teenager, exploring Point Reyes National Seashore north of San Francisco. Like many people, she backpacked maybe once a summer throughout her early adult life and then became busy with other things and eventually didn't go at all.

In her forties, while managing her landscape construction business, Carol rediscovered the joys of the day-hike: a shorter, easier form of wilderness experience. One thing lead to another and after a few years of weekend day-hikes, backpacking became possible again.

Carol found backpacking the perfect retreat from cell phones and freeways. Being older and wanting to extend her years on the trail, as well as improving the quality of those years, she proceeded to find the lightest, most comfortable gear available.

Carol now spends more than 60 nights in the wilderness under the stars each season.

Dedicated to The Light

©2008 by Carol Corbridge

All inquiries should be addressed to:
Frank Amato Publications, Inc. • P.O. Box 82112 • Portland, Oregon 97282
503-653-8108 • www.amatobooks.com

Book & Cover Design: Mariah Hinds
Artwork by Jayna Harrison
ISBN-10: 1-57188-442-4
ISBN-13: 978-1-57188-442-8
UPC: 0-81127-00277-1
Printed in Singapore

1 3 5 7 9 10 8 6 4 2

Table of Contents

Introduction
Heading into the Light

I'm a 57-year-old non-athletic woman. And I've been hitting the trail pretty hard for about 10 years now; more and more every year since I've retired in 2004. Last season, I figure I slept under the stars about 60 nights. Most trips are five or six nights long.

One nice thing about being older is I'm not a starving student anymore. My old gear from the 70's was so outdated I did the research and bought all new everything. Once I got started on this path, I was fascinated by the new technology. I kept looking for the latest, lightest and most innovative gear. And I'm a very thorough and focused person. Some would say compulsive.

I've made charts and spreadsheets. I've read everything I could find about backpacking and walking and gear. I have cruised the web. I've tried at least

Homemade Rayway Tarp and Clark Jungle Hammock set up at Lower Caribou Lake in the Trinity Alps Wilderness, CA.

10 different backpacks, from the standard to the wildly experimental. I've used wearable sleeping bags with arm holes and hiked for miles in sandals. I've slept in hammocks and created homemade sleeping bags for my dog. I've used Reflectix heating-duct insulation and beer can stoves. But that wasn't enough. I bought an old sewing machine on eBay and started modifying everything to my liking. Sometimes it worked, sometimes not so much.

I've loved every minute of it. I have an entire room at my house dedicated to gear. And I've come to some conclusions about gear and weight and function and comfort and aging.

So, here are my thoughts and my favorite gear. I've back-pedaled some from my most extreme light-weight days. I've added back the things I really want. But, I think long and hard about every ounce I put into my pack. You should too. Now I enjoy the journey as well as the destination.

What Light Can Do For You

My goal is to extend the years I can comfortably spend on the trail. Lighter loads put less stress on my body and do less damage to my aging joints. Less is more. I enjoy the simple act of walking, especially walking in beautiful places. When my pack is heavy, all I think about is the burden on my back. I think about my knees, my hips and 'are we there yet?' When my pack is light enough, I forget about it and look around. I see the view, smell the pines and hear the birds.

The average pack probably weighs around 50 pounds for a weekend trip. I find by being carefully selective I can get away with about 35 pounds for a six-night trip with a partner. This includes everything: 1.8 liters water, food, everything. And there are some luxuries included in this total. I take fly-fishing gear, a camera, a book, and swim fins. Once you get your pack weight down, you can add back those things that make the trip fun for you. A lighter pack weight does not mean skimping on fun or safety.

If you make considered decisions about your necessary gear, you will have room for a few carefully selected luxuries.

First Things First

If you want to head into lightness, buy a kitchen or postal scale. Almost any scale will do as long as it can measure fractions of ounces. The important thing is to weigh everything. This is a must. Everything that goes into your pack must be weighed. Which pants to take? Weigh them. Pick the lightest that will do the job. Pay attention to ounces. If you do, the pounds will take care of themselves.

Once you have your scale, go through your gear and weigh EVERYTHING. Did I say to weigh everything? I use a spreadsheet to keep track, but you should at least write down on a sheet of paper the weights of the things you intend to carry. Then start replacing the heavy things with lighter options.

Whether re-outfitting or starting from scratch, begin with the big things. Buy good-quality light-weight gear. Your shelter will cost you the most and save you the most weight. Don't skimp here. Decide on this component first. Then work your way through the rest.

The last thing to select is your backpack. After you have a good idea what you're going to carry, then you're ready to decide on the pack to put it all in.

One other thing I recommend to would-be load lighteners is Ray Jardine's book: *Beyond Backpacking*. This is the book that started the light-weight backpacking revolution. See recommended reading in the back for other supplemental reading.

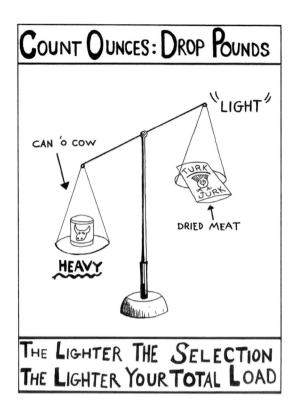

Getting Started on the Trail

If you haven't backpacked before or if you haven't in a long time, you need to start by day hiking. Find a local trail and pack a lunch and some spare clothes and give it a spin. Work your way up to carrying a full backpack. I often carry a fully loaded backpack on a day hike just to stay in shape.

This is also a good way to test out new gear. Rain gear can be tested in the shower for leaks, but there's nothing like real trail conditions. I would rather discover gear problems when I have a nice warm car at the end of the trail and my bed waiting at home than when I'm dependent on it in the wilderness. I especially like to day hike on rainy days to try out various kinds of rain wear.

How to Use This Book

The Boomer's Guide is roughly organized into sections like rooms of a house. You carry your entire house on your back. I have listed my preferred gear selections at the end of each chapter and include a compilation of them all in one big preferred gear list in Appendix A at the end of the book. These **What Works for Me** lists include weights, brands, websites and costs. The weights are manufacturers' weights when I could find them and mine when I couldn't. They can vary from unit to unit. The costs are approximate at the time of publication.

Heavy Hiker

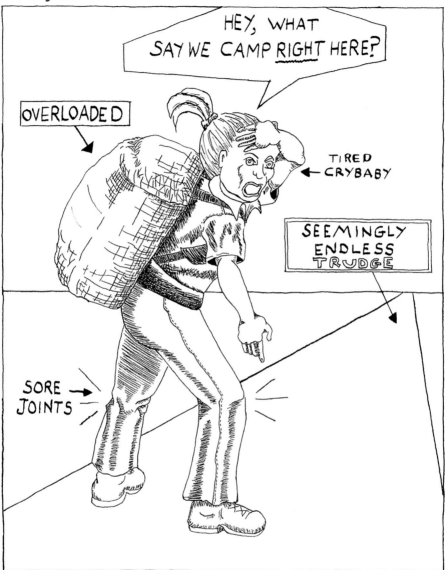

One way to go is to turn first to my **What Works for Me** charts and then backtrack for more detailed info in the associated chapter. Or you can read just an individual chapter to look at a single gear category in depth. Or go directly to The Boomer Bottom Line, my summary chapter. Or you can read the entire book from cover to cover for a complete overview of my gear selections.

So let's look into each of the rooms of your erstwhile home.

What Works For Me

Item	Oz.	Cost	Website
My Weigh Postal Scale 7001DX	NA	$35	http://myweigh.com/scales/medium-scales
Pelouze 7810 Hanging Scale	NA	$50	http://www.pelouze.com/hanging.html

Happy Hiker

 # Gimme Shelter

This is a very important component of your outfit. It is the heaviest of your gear, so a great place to save pounds. It also is your shelter. YOUR ONLY SHELTER. So it must be adequate or you will be uncomfortable at the least or dead from hypothermia at the most.

Tarp and tent, Lost Coast, CA.

Hammocks

I use a hammock. Before you announce you could never sleep in a hammock, you should know that backpacking hammocks are way better than backyard lounging hammocks. The recommended Clark Jungle Hammock Ultra Light holds up to 300 pounds. This form of backcountry sleeping is worth your consideration.

The next objection to hammocks I usually get is, "Isn't it hard to find two trees?" Well, "Isn't it hard to find a flat, rock-free spot on the ground?" If you want to camp where everyone else has for the last 50 years, then there is a flat spot on the ground. If you want to camp anywhere else, there usually isn't a flat spot. Sure, you can create one. This takes time; lots of time. It also has a major impact on the environment.

Finding two trees is fairly easy and is low impact. Your options are many, including most established campsites. This is true almost everywhere except the desert and above tree line. Sometimes a BIG rock will do as well as a tree. I most often choose somewhere away from the crowd. For instance, I go to the opposite side of the lake, where the rocks slope down into the water. There is no flat spot big enough for a tent, but there are two trees with a great view and no other people.

For the aging body, I have found the hammock to be far more comfortable than the ground. I like the stars in my eyes when I open them and only put up my tarp when rain threatens. When I used to sleep on the ground, I would take two ibuprofen every couple of hours to quiet the pain in my hips. No problems now. I sleep deeply and well. I also like the rocking motion of the hammock.

Clark Jungle Hammock at South Sugar Lake, Russian Wilderness, CA.

Hammock sleeping requires some practice. Lay diagonal to get the flattest sleeping space. Put a stuff bag of clothes under your knees, to further flatten your position.

Try different tautness hangs. Too smiley means a jackknife-like position. Too tight means your shoulders are squished into your sides. You can turn over and lay on your side comfortably, but not on your stomach. No worries about falling out. Camping hammocks are engineered to eliminate this problem.

Side sleeping in the North American by Clark Jungle Hammock.

As I've gotten older it's become harder to get up off the ground. Getting up to pee at night is much easier with a hammock. A hammock makes a great chair for reading, putting your boots on, or just lounging. Most hammocks come complete with zip-up bug screening, so bugs are not a problem.

Under-Hammock Insulation

There is one problem with hammocks. That is keeping your lower side warm. You don't need any cushioning, but you do need insulation. Your sleeping bag won't work, because you are laying on it, therefore squishing the loft into nothing or almost nothing. So your sleeping bag is used as a quilt on top of you, partly unzipped with your feet in the bottom pocket.

There are many under-layer insulation choices out there. Conventional self inflating pads, like the thermarest, work fairly well, except they are not wide enough. Wherever your body touches the hammock you will feel cold. If you lay on your back, your shoulders normally will touch and be cold. If you lay on your side, your butt will touch and be cold. I have tried many, many things to solve this problem.

One inexpensive solution that works better than most is using a section of Reflectix heating duct insulation. It comes in rolls. It's light and wide enough. It works great. Except... It's noisy when you roll around, reflects moonlight into your face while you're trying to sleep, and worst of all, is bulky. I carried it across the top of my pack. It makes a shiny metallic cylinder that looks like some kind of weird sci-fi electronic receiver.

The best solution I've found is the Under Quilt; a quilt made especially for hammock camping. You simply suspend it under the hammock by mini bunji cords and carabineers. With the under quilt the entire inside of your hammock is free for your sleeping pleasure. With any of the in-hammock solutions there is a certain amount of wrestling that goes on to get the insulation in place under your body. This sleep-disturbing situation is completely eliminated with the under quilt.

PCT near Deadfall Lakes, CA.

The No Sniveller in action under the Ultralight by Clark Jungle Hammock
at Virginia Lake, Trinity Alps Wilderness, CA.

There are a few under quilts available and they are all fairly expensive. You could take an old sleeping bag and modify it to fit under your hammock and save about $200.

One caveat: If you can't find two trees, you must "go to ground" using your hammock as a ground cloth and bivy of sorts. If you have an inflatable pad, you will be very comfortable. If you don't, you will be less comfortable. I have done this without a pad once and used leaves and other debris to soften the forest floor. Camping in less used sites usually means more duff and softer ground. Don't clear this cushioning away.

Tarps, Tents and Tarp Tents

The hammock is not the lightest option. A tarp for two with a ground cloth is by far the lightest. Next would be a single wall tent for two. Even the solo packer is better off weight-wise with a tarp or a tent than a hammock. I use a hammock because it is worth the weight to me. You will have to judge for yourself where to spend your ounces.

Tarps are harder to set up, but more versatile than tents. I like the openness of a tarp. The reason I camp is to be in nature. I find a tent confining. Some people feel safer in a tent. But, they provide only psychological comfort and no real protection from the wildlife. I feel unnecessarily cut off from my

environment in a tent. I also enjoy setting up and breaking down camp. So I would choose a tarp over a tent.

There is a new category of tents called tarp tents. They combine the openness of a tarp with the easy set up of a tent. Well worth considering. They are light-weight and well designed.

I put a tarp up over my hammock when I need shelter from the sun or rain. Most hammocks come with rain flys, but I prefer something bigger. So I use a Golite Cave 2 type tarp. I made this myself with a kit from Ray Jardine.

Happy camper in Henry Shires Tarptent Cloudburst.

The Golite Cave 2 is just like the Rayway Kit only it's ready to go, no assembly needed. These are hard to find now, since they have been discontinued by Golite. This particular design is good because it has beaks on either end on the tarp. These overhangs make more usable space in rain and wind.

If you can't find the Cave 2 and don't want to make your own, Jacks R Better makes a nice 10 x 11 tarp that's almost the same weight as the Cave 2, but has no beaks. It is somewhat larger though and that may make up for the lack of beaks.

Sleeping Bags

Once you decide on a hammock, a tent or a tarp tent, then you can finish out your shelter kit with a sleeping bag, pad or under quilt and a tarp if needed.

Buy the best sleeping bag you can afford. I have two, one for summer and one for colder weather. To achieve your lightweight goal, consider your clothing as part of your sleeping system. I always wear at least my swim clothes in my hammock. It's more comfortable for me than bare skin. Most often though, I wear silk long underwear and a fleece cap. When very cold, I wear an insulated top, insulated bottoms, down booties, gloves, etc. These are items I'm already carrying. Sleeping in them allows me to carry a lighter bag.

Homemade Rayway Tarp with bug netting.

Sleeping bag temperature ratings are not to be trusted. You can use them in comparing different bags to each other. Even then the ratings can be misleading. Loft is a good way to judge a bag. Lay it down and measure the height of the top layer only. The bottom layer doesn't really count, since you will be laying on it and flattening it. Some bags are made with very little or no insulation in the half on the bottom. They are called 'top only bags' or 'top bags'. Big Agnes makes one with a slot on the bottom that holds an insulating pad in place.

I would not even consider anything but down for a sleeping bag. It is much warmer for the weight. And down bags last longer than synthetic bags. The only advantage to a synthetic bag is that it supposedly works when it is wet. I've never had my down bag fail, even under some pretty wet conditions. It takes quite a lot to saturate a down bag. The down continues to work unless the feathers are so wet they clump together and lose their loft. I once even had puddles on the surface of my bag in insidious wet fog and stayed warm inside. I wear synthetic insulated pants in cold conditions, so I suppose that is some backup, but it's never come into play. A down bag should always be protected from the wet, whether in your pack, tent or hammock. I think down is the only way to go with a sleeping bag.

*Homemade Rayway Tarp and Clark Jungle Hammock set up at the
Lost Coast, CA. Note chimney is used as one of the 'trees'.*

Ground Pads

If using a tent or tarp on the ground, you will need a sleeping pad. This is one
area where boomers should not skimp. The best I have found are the down-
filled, inflatable pads. They have up to 3 inches of loft, pack down small and
are reasonably light. Down filling cannot be inflated by your breath due to
the moisture content. So they come with a lightweight pump bag. This can
be a hassle. There are also inflatable pads filled with synthetic insulation that
are worth considering. You can blow them up with your breath, but they are
heavier for the warmth and not as cushy.

What Works For Me

Item	Oz.	Cost	Website
AirCore PRO Guyline	1.2	$24	http://www.backpackinglight.com/ weight for 50 ft. of line
Clark Ultra Light Jungle Hammock	38.0	$179	http://www.junglehammock.com/ weight includes fly
Exped DownMat 7 Short w/pump sack	24.0	$125	http://www.exped.com
Golite Cave 2 Tarp	18.0	$120	Cave 2 discontinued, maybe find it used or as closeout
Henry Shires Tarp Tent Cloudburst w/floor	38.0	$250	http://www.tarptent.com/products.html
Jacks R Better No Sniveler Under Quilt	20.0	$250	http://www.jacksrbetter.com/
JRB 10 x 11 Cat Tarp	19.0	$120	http://www.jacksrbetter.com/
JRB Bear Mt Bridge Hammock	33.0	$200	http://www.jacksrbetter.com/
Kelty Triptease Lightline	2.5	$15	http://www.campmor.com/ weight for 50 ft. of line
Pacific Outdoor Max Ether Thermo 6 2/3 (synthetic air mat)	16.0	$75	http://www.pacoutdoor.com
Rayway Tarp Kit	19.0	$71	http://www.ray-way.com/php/order-form.php just like Cave 2 & comes with instruction book
Stephenson DAM (custom down air mat)	19.8	$140	http://www.warmlite.com/start.htm#anchor28960

Item	Oz.	Cost	Website
Titanium Tent Stakes (6)	1.5	$24	http://www.backpackinglight.com/
Western Mountaineering Highlite Sleeping Bag	16.0	$250	http://www.westernmountaineering.com/index.cfm
Western Mountaineering Megalite Sleeping Bag	24.0	$325	http://www.westernmountaineering.com/index.cfm

Relaxing in the Henry Shires Tarptent Cloudburst on an Exped DownMat 7 Short.

 # Food, Glorious Food!

Food is so good in the fresh air. Exercise creates a healthy appetite to say the least. I enjoy being hungry when camping. As a culture, affluent Americans seldom experience hunger. People almost always pack too much food.

Snack time!

I try to come close to bringing nothing home from a trip into the wild. I figure there is no way I'm going to starve. Water and temperature control are much more important to survival than food. Most Americans, me included, have a reserve of food built into their bodies and could go quite a few days without any damage. I've never had too, but I could. I don't worry about having enough food, I worry about taking too much.

Don't get me wrong. I enjoy my meals in the back country and eat at least three per day. Later in this chapter I'll talk about dialing in your food, so you don't end up taking too much. But first, let's look at the kitchen.

Stove

Some ultra light people go stoveless. I never have and probably never will. There is great comfort in warmth from without. A hot beverage in the morning gets me out of bed. A hot meal at night warms my inner body before the cold of the mountains sets in.

Waiting for water to boil in the Litech Kettle on the Titanium Sierra Zip Stove.

I've tried a few stoves from light to heavy. There are two I use depending on the conditions. There are many other choices, but these work for me.

First, and my favorite, is the Sierra Zip Stove. It's a wood-burning stove with a small fan that makes it into a mini forge. Boils water in about 3 minutes, virtually the same time as most canister stoves. But unlike canisters, the Zip Stove runs on little pieces of wood or charcoal. It has an AA battery that runs the tiny fan. It takes only a handful of twigs to make dinner or breakfast for two.

I should note that I only boil water when cooking in the wild. I use freeze-dried meals that require only boiling water and time to prepare. This way I have no pots to wash and I create less bear-attracting odors.

I like the Zip Stove because it's quiet. None of that rocket-launch sound you get with the average canister variety. And I like the Zip Stove because of the smell of the smoke and view of the fire, albeit a tiny one. I call it a little elf fire. The smoke can deter insects too.

Sometimes I use cotton balls dipped in petroleum jelly to start the little fire and sometimes dry leaves, lichen and duff from the forest floor. I carry the cotton balls in an old-style film container. This system is sweet because you don't carry those heavy fuel canisters. And you don't have to deal with the empty or partially empty canisters later. The more days you spend in the wilderness the greater the weight savings with this little stove. You do get a blackened pot from the flames, but hey you're camping, right?

The down side of this set up is getting a fire started when it's really wet and rainy. Only once did I run into a problem due to a major rain storm. I had to wait for the deluge to stop before scrounging around for dry wood. You can usually find dry wood under fallen trees or the like. I eventually got a fire going,

but I would have been much happier and had a cup of tea first thing in the morning if I had brought a JetBoil.

The JetBoil system is my choice in wet conditions. Yes, it uses a canister, but it is so easy and fast. And the most efficient of its kind, due to an integrated heat exchanger under the pot that maximizes the flame to water contact.

There are many other possibilities for lightweight systems. Alcohol stoves are exceedingly light and some people prefer them. I find them dangerous, because you can't see the flame in normal daylight conditions. They are slow. And you have to carry fuel.

The fuel-free system of the Zip Stove saved me once when my water filter failed. I was able to boil as much water as I needed without worrying about running out of fuel.

Pots and Pans

In my case this should be singular: one pot, no pans. One titanium tea kettle, actually. Holds 0.9 liters. Has a nice little folding handle and a tight-fitting lid. It is easy to pour and cute as the dickens.

I use a small plastic-covered bowl about the size of a cottage cheese container for instant oatmeal and the like, a long-handled titanium spoon and a tall plastic cup. The cup is the lightest most flexible I could find. You want something that won't break under pressure in your pack if it gets squished. I usually stuff it with socks when I pack. I don't use an insulated cup because I like to feel the warmth of the hot liquid on my hands and also insulated cups are heavier.

I also carry a classic Swiss Army Knife. You know the one, with a little pair of scissors and a toothpick.

That's it for pots, pans and dish ware.

Litech Kettle on the Titanium Sierra Zip Stove,
homemade dog bed in the background.

Food

Although I'm big on fresh food at home, I don't carry apples, carrots or any heavy low-calorie fare. Everything is as dry as possible because water is available on the trail. I add it back, rather than carry in heavy water-laden food.

Food is a very personal thing. I'm going to tell you what I've settled on, but this has evolved over 5 to 10 years and continues to change. Some of it may work for you. Some not. The general criteria will, I hope, be helpful for all.

I repackage most items in zip-locks and weigh them out to the exact serving number I need. I take extra tea and that's about it. More later on dialing in your food.

Morning

Coffee or Tea with powdered instant Soy Milk and Stevia: The coffee I use after trying many, many things is Java Juice Extract: a nitrogen-packed essence of coffee. As for tea, I sometimes pack my own in empty tea bags I buy at my local food coop. Otherwise, there are many prepacked choices. Instant soymilk is hard to find. Powdered soy milk, not so hard, but INSTANT powdered soy milk is hard. It is a great staple for me. It provides good nutrition and I like it in hot beverages. Stevia is a sugar-free natural plant derived sweetener that comes either in very concentrated liquid or powder. Lighter than sugar and much better for you.

Instant Oatmeal with Raisins and Cinnamon: I mix my own in a zip-lock and measure it out into my premarked bowl every morning.

Snacks

Clif Bars: One per day
Trail Mix: Make your own from raisins, nuts and whatever.

Lunch

Turkey Jerky, Jarlsberg Light Cheese, Fougase Bread and Crystal Light: Jarlsberg Light cheese travels better than regular full-fat cheeses and I like it better. The full-fat cheeses can separate and be quite a mess in hot weather. The bread I take is a 1-pound hard unsliced loaf that travels well too. It doesn't get moldy until day 6 or 7 if I freeze it prior to leaving. I bring lots of organic turkey jerky that I buy at Costco. Great weight-to-nutrition ratio and it can be added to freeze-dried meals in the evening as well. I use the Crystal Light individual serving packets because they're light-weight and easy.

Dinner

**MaryJanes Farm Freeze Dried Vegetarian Entrees mixed with my own
special recipe to make enough for two, sometimes Turkey Jerky and Bread
and Crystal Light**: MaryJanes Farm makes delicious meals. They are organic
and come in great variety from Curried Bisque to Red Pesto Pasta. Her
packages are burnable without leaving that foil thing. They stand up on their
own so you can use them without a bowl, just 'cooking' and eating them in the
pouch. This business was started by a forest ranger dissatisfied with the freeze-
dried food available to backpackers.

I stretch these meals by mixing in my special recipe mix.

Special Dinner - 1 serving = 3/4 cup dry:
1/2 cup	Minute Rice
2 T	Humus Mix (in bulk)
2 T	Split Pea Soup Mix (dried flakes in bulk)
3 T	Grated Dried Parmesan
2 t	Dried Onion Flakes
1/16 t	Ground Black Pepper
4-5	Sun Dried Tomatoes (dice with scissors) (dried, not in oil) (in bulk)

Use small plastic type container with lid; Add 1 cup boiling water, Stir,
Cover for 5 min; Garnish with 1 T Nutritional Yeast.

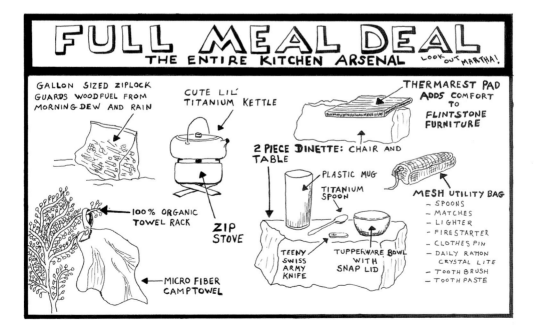

I also bring a clothes pin to close the bags while they're 'cooking'. A clothes pin can come in handy for a number of things.

Spirits

Rum: I find this to be the most palatable of spirits. At home, I'm a wine drinker, but wine is, of course, too heavy. I don't usually take any alcohol, but when I do it's rum. Once I tried taking the 151 type, figuring it would be more bang for the weight, but it was just too much bang for my taste. Of course, re-package liquid into a Platypus Little Nipper or something similar.

Dialing in your Food

First, get all the food together for a trip. Weigh everything individually on your postal or kitchen scale. Write it down. You should be doing that anyway. When you return, weigh what you bring back. Do the math and write down how much you used of each thing per day per person.

Do this on a few trips and you'll get to know what you need. Then don't worry about running out of food in the wilderness. We can go on a few less calories for a couple days if we need to. Getting hungry makes the food taste especially good, and it's a rare experience for many of us. At least that's my take on it.

I also leave some non-perishable food in the car, along with a change of clothes and some water. After the hike out, I wash up at the car and often, rather than eating yet another Clif bar, I go out for a real meal on the way home. Very fun!

Critter Protection – Bears and Others

We don't want to feed the bears, or any other animals for that matter. A fed bear is a dead bear and all that. Meaning, once they get a taste of human food they never forget. They become dangerous because they pester humans and eventually need to be destroyed.

Bear Canisters work really well and they make nifty camp chairs. But, the canisters are too heavy for my liking. Keep in mind that they're required in some human-habituated bear areas.

I used to do the bear-bag thing, throwing a rock tied to a cord over a likely tree limb. This is harder than it sounds and it is always done at the end of the day when you're tired. At least that was my excuse for not being able to hit the limb.

When I did eventually hit the limb and hoist the bag full of goodies, it never seemed high enough, or far enough from the main tree.

Since then, I've seen videos of bears making their way hand over hand out on a cord to a food bag. I think I've been pretty lucky that my food has never been ravaged considering how low and close to the tree it's been hung.

The Bear Bag Olympics – Let the games begin!

Now I use a bag made of bear-proof high-tech fabric. The originals were made with Kevlar until the war requisitioned it all. Now they're produced with some other tough-as-nails synthetic. The idea is you don't have to hang the bag. Just attach it to a tree at ground level so it can't be hauled off. This is something I can handle, even at the end of a long hot summer day.

I've never had a bear pummel my bag, but if one did the contents would be pretty messed up. This company makes a metal liner that gives the bag rigidity and minimizes mauling damage. They have had on and off approval for the habituated bear zones where canisters are required. So, when approved, you could use this instead of a canister with a substantial weight savings. Be sure to check on local regulations before setting out.

They also make a special odor-proof zip-lock thing. I found them to be not so durable and a hassle to deal with. But, under habituated bear conditions they might be worth it.

I just use the bag without the liner. I figure I'm mostly keeping rodents and raccoons out of my food. The places I hike don't have human-habituated bears. In fact, I think some of the bears I've come across have never seen a human. But, I tend to seek out solitude and off-trail destinations. In any case, this is way easier than the rock-toss Olympics.

Bear Bag, Gray Rock Lakes, Castle Crags Wilderness, CA.

What Works For Me

Item	Oz.	Cost	Website
Clif Bars	2.4	$1.25	http://www.clifbar.com/eat/eat.cfm?location=bar
Crystal Light Singles	0.6	$0.36	http://www.kraftfoods.com/CrystalLight/
Instant Soy Milk Powder	24	$6	http://www.nowfoods.com/?action=itemdetail&item_id=3493
Jarlsberg Lite Cheese	7.2	$8.10	http://www.cheesesupply.com/ or your local grocery store
Java Juice Coffee Extract	0.5	$1.20	http://www.javajuiceextract.com/
JetBoil	15.0	$70	http://www.jetboil.com/ weight without fuel
Lexan Spoon	0.3	$1.25	http://www.rei.com/product/751965
Litech 0.9 L Kettle	5.3	$20	http://www.primus.se/
MaryJanes Farm Meals	4-5	$6-8	http://products.maryjanesfarm.org/pfoshop/packages.asp
MSR Titan 2-Liter Pot	8.0	$90	http://www.msrgear.com/cookware/titan2liter.asp
Oberto Turkey Jerky Teriyaki	4.0	$5.50	http://www.obertoshopping.com/webstore/?category=149 or your local Costco
Sierra Zip Stove Regular	17.0	$57	http://zzstove.com/mcart/
Sierra Zip Stove Titanium	9.9	$129	http://zzstove.com/mcart/
Stevia Extract	0.9	$14	http://www.stevia.com/ or your local health food store
Titanium Long Handled Spoon	0.4	$13	http://www.backpackinglight.com/
Ursack Major	15	$65	http://www.ursack.com/ursack-catalog.htm

Cool Clear Water

I think the rule is 3-3-3. You can last three minutes without air; three days without water and three weeks without food. So air is pretty darned important and if you don't have that, well, none of this will really matter. So let's focus on the next most important survival basic: water. There are a few ways to purify your water. And nowadays you had better purify it just about everywhere.

Pumping water with the MSR Miniworks at Diamond Lake, Trinity Alps Wilderness, CA.

Filtering

I use a filter pump. It's heavier than some methods, but I like my water clear and now. Some methods, like drops, make water safe to drink but leave it cloudy and nasty tasting. Drops also require waiting up to an hour. A pump doesn't require waiting, only the time it takes to pump. I can pump from even a mud puddle and get nice sweet clear water in just a few minutes.

The new infrared red light purifiers, although faster than the drops, have the same problem with the turbidity. And I'm not sure how fragile the bulbs are either.

I use a filter with a ceramic element housed in a hard plastic pump. The element is made of a material like a clay flower pot that can be scrubbed with a kitchen scrubby and then rinsed off to clear the surface of small silt particles. This is known as being field cleanable. The only down side to this filter, other than its weight, is one could drop the ceramic filter when cleaning it and break it. I'm really careful when cleaning. I also wrap a coffee cone filter around the intake and secure it with a rubber band to pre-filter the water when it's really dirty. This minimizes the need for field cleaning.

MSR is coming out with the new Hyperflow in spring 2008. It looks interesting; doing everything the Miniworks does at three times the speed and half the weight. Except, according to their website, it does not remove the taste and odor of chemicals and toxins. I'm not sure what that means. They say, don't pump out of mining tailing pools or large agricultural operations. Good idea, no matter what.

Always test your filter before each trip and clean and dry it after each trip. Check all the fittings and gaskets. Lubricate as needed.

There is a new no-mix, short-wait product in the drops category called Klearwater. It's much lighter than a pump. I will give it a try next season when I know water will be plentiful and clear. You only need to wait 15 minutes with this tasteless clear liquid. When I have a chance of encountering cloudy water I'll stick with the heavier pump though.

Platypus 1.8-liter Hoser is my water container of choice.

Hydration Bladders and Water Containers

Bladders make water available to you without stopping on the trail. They are the lightest way to carry water. Your filter connects directly to the input hose for easy refill. They are cheap. They do fail sometimes. Check unit before each trip.

In addition to a bladder, I bring a used water or soft drink bottle. They're light and last for a trip usually. Handy for extra water and for use around camp or for short day hikes. I use it like a canteen. The small ones fit in my pants cargo pockets for day hikes or fishing when I don't want to take my pack.

For water storage at camp I carry a six-liter Platypus Water Tank. I pump it full when I get to camp and then two of us are good until the next morning after coffee.

What Works For Me

Item	Oz.	Cost	Website
MSR Miniworks	16.0	$85	http://www.msrgear.com/watertreatment/miniworks.asp
Platypus 1.8 L Hoser	3.5	$20	http://www.platypushydration.com/
Platypus 6 L Water Tank	3.5	$20	http://www.platypushydration.com/
KlearWater by Xinix	2.9	$8	http://www.backpackinglight.com/

4 The Clothes on Your Back

Clothing is your first level of shelter in the wilderness. Clothing selection needs to be done very carefully. It's all about regulating the temperature of your body. Multi-use gear is important, as is layering. I try to select the lightest set of clothing that will keep me comfortable in all the conditions I'm likely to encounter. And then add one more layer for extra credit.

Embracing the view, Sawtooth Ridge, Trinity Alps Wilderness, CA.

Remembering to *always* consider weight, I only take one of everything except socks. I take two pair of socks. I don't take underwear. If I did, I would take only two pair of them too no matter how long I was out.

I don't worry about getting dirty. Getting dirty is part of the experience for me. Sometimes, in nice weather, I rinse out clothes or just go swimming with them on to wash them. But in cool or wet weather things just get dirty. I worry much more about keeping things dry than keeping them clean.

Our bodies sweat to cool us down. This works quite well. This is also the reason we should not take cotton clothing backpacking. It dries very slowly. Often after our bodies have cooled down, cotton clothing is still wet from exercise.

Morning comfort wearing the Exped Wallcreeper Sleeping Bag with arm holes and cinch bottom & Marmot Precip Full Zip Rain Pants.

Then the cool-down effect is a problem; we start to get cold. Clothing for backpacking needs to dry quickly so it can warm as well as cool our bodies.

Rain Gear

Speaking of keeping things dry, I always take rain-gear. Even just for a single night with a clear forecast. This is partly because I wear my rain-gear bottoms almost every morning; one more abrasion-resistant layer over my sleeping outfit. But also because it can rain any time in the mountains. Getting wet is the first step toward hypothermia.

I usually take full-side-zip pants. This is one of the places I've added back some weight to my kit. I own lighter, less durable rain pants, but they only get packed in the warmest of conditions as an emergency backup when it seems very unlikely I'll need them. The really ultralight rain gear, especially the pants, don't last very long in the real world.

Durability isn't such a big deal in a rain top, since you don't sit on it. So I use some pretty lightweight rain tops. They double as a windbreaker, but I don't wear them every morning, like I do the pants.

Ready for rain, Oregon Coast.

Although I always take rain gear, I've found that no rain gear really works very well when you're exercising. The sweat your body produces needs to escape or it condenses inside the gear. Result: even if your gear doesn't leak, you are wet.

So breathe-ability and venting are important in rain gear. This is another good reason for the full-zip pants. The zippers provide venting and ease when putting them on/off over boots. There is a constant parade of new breathable fabrics that started with Gore-Tex. They all work to some degree and tend to be expensive. Zippered mesh pockets can work as vents too. But too many pockets and zippers add weight. Remember, most of the time your rain gear is in your pack.

This weight-versus-function issue turns up over and over again. I have gotten down to the absolute minimum weight on most things and then carefully decided where to add back weight in favor of function, comfort or luxury.

I actually carried a very light umbrella for an entire summer. Wonderful venting and it provides sun protection too. The idea was that it replaced my rain top. But on the down side it requires at least one hand and was useless in the wind. I ultimately decided its uses were too limited.

Remember to size your rain gear large, to go over layers and allow freedom of movement. Extra space aids ventilation too.

Poncho at Sugar Pine Lake, Trinity Alps Wilderness, CA.

Boots

I've tried many, many boots. Your feet are your only means of transport and can't be pampered too much. Comfort is prime here. Weight can be part of comfort to a degree. Remember you have to lift your feet and your boots over and over again. My trail shoes are so comfortable that I'm happy to wear them around camp. They are waterproof and breathable. They are what is known as lightweight hikers or glorified sneakers.

Fit is personal and can even be different from your right to left foot. Some rules of thumb, or toe in this case, are as follows. A large foot box is important. This means room for your toes to move around a bit and swell as your feet work. At the same

Gear adjustments, off trail, Trinity Alps Wilderness, CA.

time, you want your heel to be snug and not move within your shoe as you walk. Also good arch support is necessary. I use after-market Hapad inserts that mold to my high arch. Take your inserts with you when trying on shoes. When you do find the perfect hiking boot, buy a couple pairs, because they are sure to be discontinued.

Camp Shoes

I use a Croc-like shoe. It goes on the outside of my pack for water crossings. I swim in them and sometimes wear them around camp. They have a full heel and strap on securely enough I could hike in them if I had to. I actually use them around camp for short walks and minor exploring. They are great for fishing and wading too.

Pants

I take one pair of synthetic zip-off hiking pants. I was surprised at how much difference there was in the weight of my various pants, so be sure to weigh your choices. The zip-off needs to be of the light plastic kind and at both leg and ankle, so you can get the legs off over boots.

Your pants and all your clothing must be cotton free. Repeat: no cotton. Not even in a blend. Cotton takes forever to dry. And even a small amount of cotton in a blend will prolong the drying time of that garment considerably. A wet garment is a cold garment. This limits multi use.

Off trail in the Trinity Alps Wilderness.

I always wear cargo pants. Very handy on the trail. The pockets need to be on the side of the leg, not the front. On the front they impede every step you take and as you walk your leg swings right into the pocket contents. This gets very annoying on step number 568. The cargo pockets should be bellowed. I like deep-slash pockets on the sides and at least one zipper pocket for security. Back pockets aren't necessary and sometimes can be a problem if they are where your pack rides. I've removed buttons when this happens.

Swimwear

Swimwear is not strictly necessary in the wilderness where skinny dipping is the norm. But, just in case, I carry very lightweight running shorts and a tank top that can double as a swim top. These garments also can be used to sleep in and as a back-up if something happens to your main shirt and pants, or you're washing them.

Long Underwear

Tops and bottoms are a great layering item. My hiking pants are light weight and long underwear bottoms are needed when it's cold. They also make great sleepwear.

I use either silk, synthetic, merino wool or a combination fabric depending on the conditions. Most often I take the silk which is the lightest and most comfortable; warm when it's cold and cool when it's hot. They also dry quickly.

Gloves

I have tried many gloves. My hands tend to get cold easily and, like rain gear, I've found nothing that really

Lakeside at Lake Anna,
Trinity Alps Wilderness, CA.

works all the time. So I carry chemical pack hand warmers that heat up when exposed to air. I put them inside my gloves next to the back of my hands where the blood flows to my fingers. These last 4-6 hours and do the trick, but they are heavy.

I use Possumdown gloves with silk liners. Both are light-weight. Possumdown is a material made in New Zealand. It's advertised as the second highest warmth-to-weight ratio on the planet. Goose down is first. It's actually a blend of possum fur and merino wool. Very soft and water resistant. Not very durable though. They last about a year for me; I'm on my third pair.

I've tried a few waterproof coverings for my gloves. Event is a good fabric for this application. It works better than most, but, like all rain gear, it doesn't work very well. It's not the fabric's fault, it's the big hole in every glove where your hand goes in that's the problem. I find I have to take my gloves on and off for various activities and that allows water to infiltrate the inner sanctum.

Socks

I probably take too many pairs of socks, but my feet are important to me. I take two pair of hiking socks and one pair of Possumdown sleeping socks. Possumdown isn't durable enough to wear with shoes, but it is a delight to put on for sleeping. In any case you should never sleep in the socks you've been wearing all day. They are damp and that dampness translates into cold. So always put on a fresh pair of socks when you go to bed. If you only have two pair of socks just rotate them. Possumdown is a wonderful lightweight luxury.

Hats and Headwear

For body temperature control a hat is indispensable. I take a couple of hats or cowls. A cowl or balaclava is a good layering item. I have an assortment and take different weights for different weather conditions.

Most often for warmth I take a silk balaclava, a synthetic buff and a fleece stocking or watch cap. Sometimes I take a convertible balaclava/watch cap that's heavier but warmer.

Possumdown Sweater and Balaclava, very versatile.

For sun I usually take a Tilley hat. I've also used a Sunday Afternoon hat which I liked very much. It wads up in my pack with no problems. For rain I usually take a shower cap like thing that goes over my Tilley hat. I found this on a police hat website. It's called a campaign hat rain cover. It works really well and is light, of course.

If your rain jacket has a hood then you may not need a rain hat. I hate hoods, because they block my hearing and sight. The Tilley hat arrangement is more vented than a hood allowing air to flow freely. I sometimes wear a silk balaclava or my buff with my Tilley to keep my ears warm.

I also carry a bug head net. It's light and when I need it, I really need it. It can go over or under my hat and it is black, so my vision is not so obscured as by

Tilley LTM6 Hat.

a lighter color. The one I use is spendy, you can buy one for a fraction of the cost that will certainly get you by.

Hiking Shirts

This item needs to provide sun protection and work well with a pack. I like to use the coolest possible shirt, so mine has mesh vents all along the sides and a vent flap on the back. I like long sleeves for the sun protection, but with the option to roll them up. I like button-up for further venting and all synthetic material. Absolutely no cotton.

Warmth Layers -Top Side

This is an area where versatility is important. I have a Possumdown sweater that always makes the cut. Light, breathable, warm, water resistant and so comfortable.

Bug Head Net, Ursack and K9 Topcoats.

After three days of rain everything needed to be aired out. Boy, was that sun nice! Kalmiopsis Wilderness, OR.

I also take a down vest and a synthetic insulated pullover. Along with my silk long underwear and rain top I'm able to mix and match to meet most conditions. In colder shoulder seasons I bring merino wool blend long underwear instead of silk.

Warmth Layers – Bottom Side

When walking I seldom wear anything on my lower body, but my hiking pants. When it's really cold sometimes I wear my long underwear. But around camp I need something more, so I bring synthetic insulated pants. They are way too hot to hike in, but super warm and light. I usually wear my rain pants over them, since they aren't very durable; kind of like wearing a sleeping bag on your legs.

As with the top side, in the colder shoulder seasons I bring merino wool blend long underwear instead of silk.

Extra Credit – Feet

Down Booties

Some might consider these a luxury item, but I like my feet toasty, so I carry down booties. They are for sleeping, although I sometimes wear them in the

*Montebell Thermawrap Jacket, Ursack, Platypus Water Tank,
Dog, Kalmiopsis Wilderness, OR.*

morning if the ground is dry. Chemical heat packs also work wonders on cold feet in bed.

Gaiters

I always wear gaiters. Short ones that keep the little rocks and leaves out of my boots. Most often I use ones made from eVent, a waterproof breathable fabric. They are light, cool and every time I don't wear them, I'm sorry. I hate stuff in my shoes and since I go off trail often, I'm a high-risk shoe-debris candidate.

As a final word on clothing, I use my clothing as a booster for my sleeping bag. If I bring my summer sleeping bag and find myself in a surprise cold spell, I wear all my clothing to bed. This is more comfortable than it sounds, especially if you carry clothing you've selected with this in mind. I often go to bed wearing more clothing than I need. It's easier to take off clothes to cool down rather than trying to warm up once you're cold.

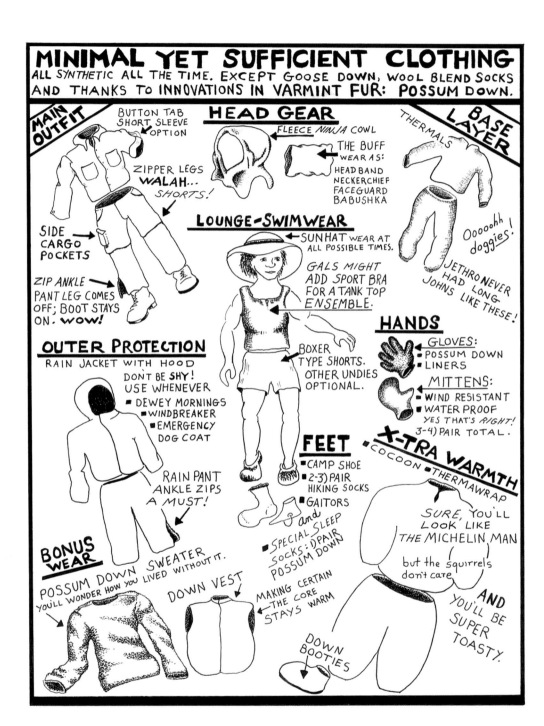

Sunglasses and Readers

I like my eyes protected. Polarization and rose tint improve the view of the sky, clouds and water. These are my preferences. I also fly-fish, so polarized glasses are a must.

Being a boomer, I need reading glasses and I bring two pair. One I keep handy for map reading, etc., the other is stashed in my pack as backup. I get the lightest I can find. They can get trashed on the trail so I replace them regularly.

What Works For Me

Item	Oz.	Cost	Website
BPL Bug Head Net	0.33	$20	http://www.backpackinglight.com/
Campmor Bug Head Net	0.5	$5	http://www.campmor.com/
Clear Campaign Hat Rain Cover for Tilley	1.0	$6	http://www.mtuniforms.com/catalog/index.php?cPath=25
Cocoon UL 60 Pants	6.9	$180	http://www.backpackinglight.com/
Cocoon UL 60 Pullover	8.6	$190	http://www.backpackinglight.com/
Costco Reading Glasses	0.5	?	Comes in a (3) pack and is not available online
Dahlgren Hiking Socks	3.3	$17	http://www.dahlgrenfootwear.com/hiking.shtml
Driducks Rain Pants and Jacket	12.0	$20	http://www.froggtoggs.com/ Light, cheap, breathable, but not so durable. Good emergency rain gear.
FF Down Booties	9.0	$85	http://www.featheredfriends.com/
Frogg Toggs Pants	6.5	$45	http://www.froggtoggs.com/ cost for entire suit (pants not sold separately)
Frogg Toggs Pro Action Jacket	9.5	$45	http://www.froggtoggs.com/ cost for entire suit (jacket not sold separately)
Hand Warmer Packs	1.5	$1.50	http://www.warmers.com/default.aspx
Hapad Comf-Orthotic Sport Insoles w/ Scaphoid Pads	2.3	$20	http://www.hapad.com/hapadonline/home.php?cat=267 & http://www.hapad.com/hapadonline/home.php?cat=280
Icebreaker Bodyfit 200 Leggings	7.3	$60	http://www.icebreaker.com/
Icebreaker Bodyfit200 Mondo Zip Long Sleeve Top	9.3	$70	http://www.icebreaker.com/

Item	Oz.	Cost	Website
ID eVent Shortie Gaiters	2.5	$30	http://www.integraldesigns.com/
ID Hot Socks	4.5	$45	http://www.integraldesigns.com/
Insport 5K Shorts	2.9	$20	http://www.insport.com/products.cfm?main_id=1&sub_id=1
Loki Hat	2.0	$25	http://www.lokiusa.com/product_detail.php?ID=H201#
Marmot Precip Full Zip Rain Pant	10.0	$90	http://marmot.com/
Merrell Moab Mid GTX XCR Hikers	31.0	$120	http://www.merrell.com/
MLD eVent Rain Mitts	0.9	$45	http://www.mountainlaureldesigns.com/shop/index.php
Montebell U.L. Thermawrap Pants	10.3	$130	http://www.montbell.us/products/list.php?cat_id=75
Montebell U.L. Thermawrap Parka	12.8	$165	http://www.montbell.us/products/list.php?cat_id=73
Mountain Hardwear Hyperdry Long Sleeve Zip T	6.0	$40	http://www.mountainhardwear.com/
OR Ninjaclava	1.8	$24	http://www.outdoorresearch.com/site/ninjaclava.html
Patagonia Micro Puff Jacket	18.0	$180	http://www.patagonia.com/ or if you can find the discontinued Micro Puff Pullover, it's about half the price and lighter
Patagonia Spraymaster Rain Jacket	10.5	$300	http://www.patagonia.com/
Payless Shoes Clogs	10.0	$15	http://payless.resultspage.com/search?w=clogs
Possumdown Gloves	1.3	$30	http://www.backpackinglight.com/
Possumdown Socks	1.5	$30	http://www.backpackinglight.com/

Item	Oz.	Cost	Website
Possumdown Leather Detail Crew Neck Jumper	9.0	$190	http://www.tapestryknitwear.com/homesml.asp
Railriders Lattitude Shirt	9.0	$64	http://www.railriders.com/
SD Down Sleepies	?	$30	http://sierradesigns.com/mens.display.php?id=788
Suncloud Polarized Sunglasses	0.75	$50	www.suncloudsunglasses.com/
Sunday Afternoons Adventure Hat	3.0	$38	http://www.sundayafternoons.com/index.cgi
Tilley Hat LTM6 Airflo	4.0	$60	http://www.tilley.com/
Western Mountaineering Flight Vest	5.5	$170	http://www.westernmountaineering.com/
White Sierra Trail Convertible Pants	14.8	$35	http://www.whitesierra.com/
Wintersilks Basic Long John Crew Neck	3.7	$20	http://www.wintersilks.com
Wintersilks Lightweight Basic Long Johns	4.3	$20	http://www.wintersilks.com/
Wintersilks Spunsilk Balaclava	1.3	$14	http://www.wintersilks.com/
Wintersilks Silk/Wool Glove Liners	0.8	$13	http://www.wintersilks.com

5

Bathroom Basics

There are entire books written on this subject. Really. So I'll just cover the basics and leave the more in-depth research to you. I use as little 'product' as possible. That means soap, hand sanitizer, toilet paper and toothpaste.

Pooping and Peeing

It is important to remember the "leave no trace" ethic when answering the call of nature. Leave no trace means just that. Leave things as you find them. In no way degrade the experience of those to follow. See Appendix B, Leave No Trace Principles.

If you must use toilet paper, pack it out or burn it. Burying it doesn't work very well. It takes a long time to decompose and forest critters will dig it up. They are persistent and resourceful when it comes to finding human waste. Nothing ruins a beautiful setting like used toilet paper. If you burn it, only do so under safe conditions. I usually have a small trash-burning fire once every few days. I save my burnable trash in a zip-lock bag and burn it when it gets full and the conditions are safe. Tampax and the like get the same treatment as toilet paper.

For peeing, I use a pee rag: a piece of a camp towel or bandana. This goes on the outside of my pack to be dried by the wind and cleansed by the sun. Solar rays kill many bacteria. I also wash this item out regularly. Men have a distinct advantage in this department.

REI trowel.

Pooping requires special consideration. Only poop at least 200 feet away from any water source. Always dig a hole at least six inches deep. I carry a plastic trowel for this job. It comes in handy for other things sometimes too. My trowel broke and it now is lighter and works just as well with the shorter blade.

As a substitute for toilet paper I often use leaves. There are some soft furry ones that work great. This eliminates the problem of burning in dry conditions, since you can just bury the leaves in your six-inch, or deeper, cat hole. It is important to know your plant identification though, poison oak makes a terrible toilet paper substitute. I've heard of other TP substitutes like smooth rocks, snow, tree bark, etc. Be creative.

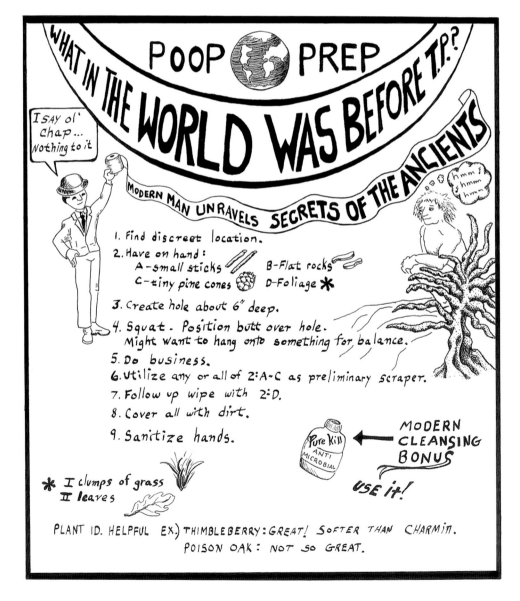

Hand Sanitizer

I think this product should not be used routinely at home. But, in the wilderness, it's a good way to keep clean. Hand washing isn't always possible. A small bottle of sanitizer is a good idea. I use it after pooping or peeing and before eating.

Grooming

I carry a small toothbrush and tooth powder. Baking soda works too.

I don't carry a brush or comb. I braid my hair before setting out and that's it. I keep a brush at the car and deal with my hair when I change into my car clothes at the trailhead. I don't carry shampoo although I wash my hair in lakes and streams sometimes, weather permitting. I do so soap free.

I carry a small container of eye drops. My eyes get dry in the mountains, so I use this to keep them lubricated.

I do carry a small amount of camp suds, a biodegradable environmentally friendly soap product. It is for washing dishes. I almost never use it. When I do, it's well away from water sources.

I don't carry a mirror for grooming, although sometimes there's one in my safety kit. It can be used for signaling potential rescuers. Makeup, body creams, deodorant, etc. all are not a good idea in the wilderness. For one thing, they can attract bears.

The one must-take body product is sunscreen. You want a fragrance-free, waterproof, sweat-proof, high-SPF product. Carry only what you need, not the giant economy size. Either re-package or buy small sizes. Fragrance-free lip balm with sunblock is another important item.

Meds

Part of aging is medications. Take with you only what you need. Depending on the criticalness of your meds, you might want to take a couple days extra, just in case.

What Works For Me

Item	Oz.	Cost	Website
MSR Packtowl UL	0.7	$10	http://www.msrgear.com/camptowels/ultralite.asp
REI Trowel	2.0	$2	http://www.rei.com/product/407146
Tooth Powder	NA	NA	Check out your local health food store or just use baking soda

6

Safety Kit

Again, there are entire books written on this subject. You should read at least one. I recommend **98.6 Degrees: The Art of Keeping Your Ass Alive** by Cody Lundin. Its premise is survival means keeping your body temperature stable. Nothing is more important. Most people who die in the wilds, die of what used to be called exposure. Now called hyper and hypo thermia. Being too cold or too hot. I am constantly trying to anticipate my body's clothing needs. I take off my sweater BEFORE climbing the hill. I put my sweater back on at the top, BEFORE I get cold.

Stream crossing, Trinity Alps Wilderness, CA.

The old safety kit was based on the boy scout motto: 'Be Prepared'. It had everything for every possibility. My safety kit only has things for the most likely issues I am going to face. That means lots of pain reliever, duct tape and band-aids. If you've ever had a car or workshop safety kit you know these are the things that go first. I like ibuprofen because it addresses muscle inflammation as well as pain and fever.

RUM: MULTIPLE USES

IT'S NOT JUST FOR TODDIES ANYMORE

■ FIRESTARTER

KEEP SAFE DISTANCE

■ ANTISEPTIC

OUCH!

FEEL THE CLEANSING ACTION

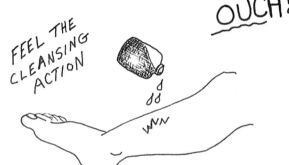

■ BATTLE MORNING BREATH

ahh... BRACING

SWISH IT!

TIP: DILUTE 151 OR SAY GOODBYE TO TASTEBUDS

Contents

I carry antibiotic ointment, fungicide ointment, duct tape, two disposable, adjustable flame, see-through lighters, a few trick birthday candles that don't blow out, Air Force fire-starting kit, spare book matches, electric tape, syringe for irrigating wounds, tiny Swiss army knife (with scissors, tweezers, toothpick, file, blade), tiny motel sewing kit (with needles and thread, free at most motels) dental floss, prescription codeine, a couple of Q tips, about ten assorted safety pins. All this fits into a quart zip-lock.

Log crossing Big French Creek, CA.

On a cord around my neck, I wear a whistle and a tiny flashlight. I only take this off when swimming. The whistle would be fantastic if I ever got lost. Much better than yelling; louder and easier to keep up for a while. Three blasts means help! I also carry another small flashlight in my pack and a head lamp. That's three light sources.

I include spare batteries and a small inflatable pad-repair kit in my safety kit.

You'll notice I have many ways to start fire. I think this is of prime importance. Truly a life-and-death issue. I put these ways to start fire in different parts of my kit. One lighter is always in my pocket as is one book of matches in a tiny zip-lock to keep them dry. Fire is not only important to keep you warm, but it also provides huge psychological comfort in the face of adversity.

Surprise snow in September, Foster Lake, Trinity Alps Wilderness, CA.

If you find yourself in a dangerous situation, the most important thing is what not to do. Don't panic. Stop and evaluate your situation, then and only then, act. Most people are rescued within three days.

Remember the rule of three. You can go without air for 3 minutes. You can go without water for three days. You can go without food for three WEEKS! Your main concern should be body temperature and mental state. Fire can help with both. I always have multiple ways to build a fire.

If you find yourself in a situation where you need water, but you have no way to treat it, by all means, drink it. It's better to be hydrated. Take your chances on contamination.

My little knife is always in my pocket too. And of course, my safety necklace is always around my neck. I go through my safety kit before every trip to replenish used items and re-think what I need.

Hiking Sticks

Everyone should use these babies, especially the over-50 crowd. They improve stability. Four legs are better than two. They give your arms some exercise. No more swollen hands. They give your knees a break. Down hills are not a big deal with a pair of sticks. They also can be used to knock rattlers out of the way and scare off the occasional cougar.

Trekking poles really help on the down hill.

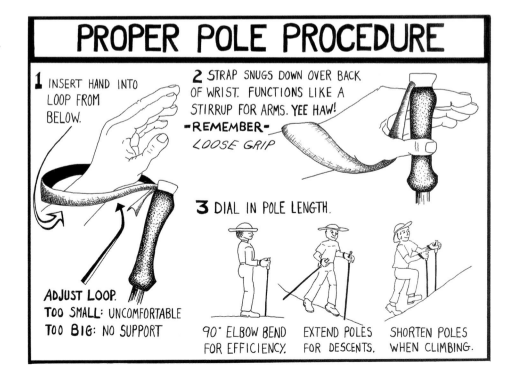

PROPER POLE PROCEDURE

1 INSERT HAND INTO LOOP FROM BELOW.

2 STRAP SNUGS DOWN OVER BACK OF WRIST. FUNCTIONS LIKE A STIRRUP FOR ARMS. YEE HAW!
-REMEMBER-
LOOSE GRIP

ADJUST LOOP.
TOO SMALL: UNCOMFORTABLE
TOO BIG: NO SUPPORT

3 DIAL IN POLE LENGTH.

90° ELBOW BEND FOR EFFICIENCY.

EXTEND POLES FOR DESCENTS.

SHORTEN POLES WHEN CLIMBING.

Are you convinced yet? I know, some people think they are for doddering old people. Well, that's right, they are. But, they're also for young through hikers who have figured out that they can go much farther in a day with the help of these. And they're for ultra-lighters who need them for their shelter set-ups. They're also for people who ford streams or go off trail and have to navigate difficult terrain.

I use them whenever I backpack. I take at least one when I day hike. The ones I use collapse, so I can strap them on my pack if so inclined.

I've never done that, but I could. They do get in the way sometimes when scrambling on all fours up a very steep rock face. But this is only for a couple of minutes and I just let them hang on my wrists by the strap. The poles are adjustable and I make them longer when I'm going down hill and shorter for steep ascents.

I like the shock absorber kind that have a little spring in them, making it easier on the wrist. Wearing them properly is very important to their function. They take about one hike to get used to and then their use becomes automatic. The poles disappear into the act of walking. Lightness is important here too.

What Works For Me

Item	Oz.	Cost	Website
ACR 0.2 oz Emergency Whistle	0.2	$3	http://www.backpackinglight.com/
Petzl E+LITE Headlamp	1.0	$30	http://en.petzl.com/petzl/LampesProduits?Produit=607 weight without carrying case
Petzl Tikka XP Headlamp	3.4	$50	http://en.petzl.com/petzl/LampesGammes?Gamme=48
Photon X-Micro LED Light	0.3	$5	http://www.backpackinglight.com/
REI Peak UL Carbon Shocklight Trekking Poles	13.5	$150	http://www.rei.com/product/750835
Spark-Lite Firestarting Kit	0.2	$10	http://www.backpackinglight.com/
Swiss Army Knife Classic SD	0.75	$16.50	http://www.swissarmy.com/
Syringe for irrigating wounds	?	free	Ask for one at your local pharmacy

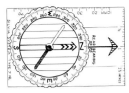

7

Get Oriented

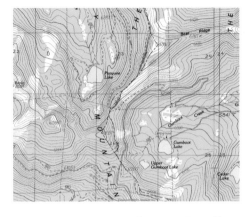

I've used a map and compass for years. I always bring at least one map, usually more. I love maps and study them both at home and in camp. While hiking, I constantly try to identify landmarks and watch for side trails, marked or unmarked, on or off the map.

Map & Compass

I take just a simple compass. I keep it readily available and use it often.

I have a computer program that can print out a 1:24 map for anywhere I hike. I use waterproof paper and print on both sides. I also take a bigger map, usually of the wilderness area I'm entering. In the car, I carry a National Forest map of the local forest. Map and compass are necessities.

GPS

Recently I purchased a GPS, so far I'm not impressed. Staring at a little computer seems to remove me from my environment. This goes against the whole reason I backpack.

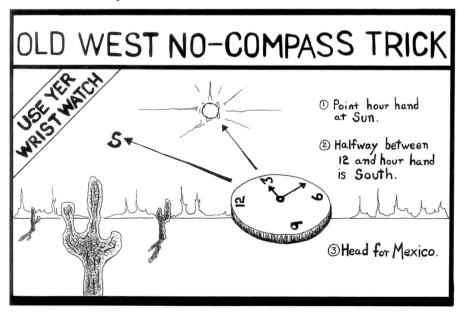

OLD WEST NO-COMPASS TRICK

USE YER WRIST WATCH

① Point hour hand at Sun.

② Halfway between 12 and hour hand is South.

③ Head for Mexico.

I am something of a computer nerd at home. I like gadgets and technology, and I can see some good features to the little GPS unit. For instance, it can leave a breadcrumb trail back to a chosen starting point. For off-trail use this could come in handy. And I do quite a lot of off-trail hiking. I first hike the trails. Then after being fairly oriented to the area I start picking off-trail routes and destinations. Amazingly often, I find old abandoned trails along these routes.

Looking back, only once did I find myself in a situation where the GPS would have been nice. I was backtracking from a day hike to an off-trail lake and missed a 90-degree turn to return to base camp. I ended up back-tracking again and refound my way, but it could have been a long walk to my bail-out point.

I always have a bail-out, or worst case scenario plan. In this case, it was to continue down hill until we hit the road. We were day hiking from a base camp, so this would have meant abandoning our camp and hiking to the car, where I always stash a set of keys. It was something like seven miles to the car, cross

Gadget Girl

country this might have taken quite a while. A GPS breadcrumb trail would have made this a non issue.

I'll continue to carry my GPS this season, at least for awhile. I'm not sure if it will make the cut as the season progresses.

PLB

I carried a Personal Locator Beacon for awhile. They are a single-use device. You pull the lever when you are in need of help. It sends out a distress signal and, depending on the unit, a GPS location. I sold it after a season. I almost always hike with a partner, so the chances of needing this unit are slim. It would only be necessary when both people were unable to get help. Two broken ankles or legs, not a very likely situation.

If you hike alone to remote locales, this might be a worthwhile investment. Alone you could break an ankle and be unable to get to help. Not too far-fetched a scenario. I would consider this if I was a routine solo hiker. They weigh about the same as a GPS, and I think they make the people at home worry less.

A PLB is certainly not a substitute for good judgment and safe hiking practices. Some are lulled into a false sense of security. Don't make that mistake.

What Works For Me

Item	Oz.	Cost	Website
ACR Electronics Terrafix 406 GPS I/O PLB	12.0	$550	http://www.acrelectronics.com/terrafix/
Adventure Waterproof Inkjet Paper	0.4	$20	http://shop.nationalgeographic.com/ product/659/3911/190.html
Brunton Classic Compass	1.1	$15	http://www.brunton.com/product.php?id=116
Garmin Vista HCx GPS	5.5	$300	https://buy.garmin.com/shop/shop. do?cID=145&pID=8703
Maptech Terrain Navigator Maps	na	$100	http://www.maptech.com/land/ cost is per state

8

Luxury Items

These are the things that just make your trip into the wilderness more fun. Sure you could do without them, but now that you've whittled down your load, there's room for some toys.

Sunday Afternoon's Adventure Hat and thrift store flippers at
Salmon Lake, Trinity Alps Wilderness, CA.

Camera

I bring a point-and-shoot light-weight 35 mm. Great entertainment value. It makes me more involved in the visual aspects of the back country. You might want to consider a waterproof model for obvious reasons. I've plunked mine in the drink a few times while fishing.

Binoculars

I have a very nice pair of compact binoculars. I love the wildlife. Many birds and bears have been enjoyed though these fine optics.

Books

Reading in the evenings is a true pleasure. But, I try to take only what I will actually read. And only paperbacks are allowed. Even among paperbacks there is a wide variety of weights, so as with everything, check it out on the scales. My hiking partner and I have an agreement to each bring a book the other has not read, so we can swap. An especially long book can be cut into sections for a trip. Put duct tape on the spine to keep the pages in place.

Games

Games can be fun too. Pick your favorite. A deck of cards or a hacky sack or a Frisbee. Frisbees, by the way, make nice dog bowls.

I bring a homemade backgammon set. It's a cloth board and plastic pieces and dice. I've played many a game lakeside.

There are mini decks of cards and chess sets etc., but I find them too small for my old eyes. If your eyes are good, maybe they would work for you.

Homemade backgammon, Platypus Hoser, Maryjanes Farm dinner, Payless camp shoes, it doesn't get any better than this!

Water Toys

Swimming in a high-mountain lake is one of the best experiences the wilderness has to offer. Most people just jump in and call it good. I have flippers and a floaty. I use an ultra-light thermarest seat as a floatation device. It is only 3.5 ounces and I use it as a seat on the trail too. It's always on the outside of my pack. It makes my butt happy.

The flippers are pretty darn heavy, but they make the cut because of the joy I get from doing laps around the largest of lakes. I'm not a very good swimmer so the floaty and fins are well worth the weight to me.

Fly-Fishing

My latest passion is fly-fishing. I bring a light-weight rod tube with my 3-or-4 piece rod cushioned by socks at either end. I carry two light fly boxes and the flies are light by their very nature. A neck pouch contains my assorted tiny tools and lines. My reel is light as well. This is a 5-weight outfit and has provided me with hours of pleasure lakeside.

I use a little gadget that attaches to my sunglasses for knot tying and hook threading. I've tried a number of these doodads, and the Flip 'n' Focus is the best. Like it sounds, it clips on your sunglasses and flips down when you need magnification and up when you don't. It also creates a very geeky look favored by fly-fishermen everywhere.

As the light fades, fishing improves, but my eyesight degrades. I then quickly change to my yellow polarized glasses with the flip focals attached; even geekier than with regular sunglasses. I always wear glasses when fishing, both for vision and safety. Flinging that hook around can get dangerous.

Fly-fishing at Lower Caribou Lake, Trinity Alps Wilderness, CA.

I'm sure there are some things you will want to bring that I haven't listed. And some things I've listed you don't want to carry so get your toys and weigh them, and then decide.

What Works For Me

Item	Oz.	Cost	Website
BPL Ultralight Fishing Rod Case	3.5	$18	http://www.backpackinglight.com/
Canon Powershot SD750	4.6	$250	http://www.usa.canon.com/
Flip 'n' Focus	0.8	$15	http://www.fishermaneyewear.com/ weight includes protective cover
Light Flippers	NA	NA	http://www.swimoutlet.com/ I got mine at a Thrift Store
Mayfly Fresh Water Pouch Lanyard	3.0	$35	http://www.mayflyhex.com/
Orvis Battenkill Bar Stock III	3.5	$120	http://www.orvis.com/
Pentex Optio W30	5.6	$275	http://www.pentaximaging.com/products/cameras/digital/
Smith Undertow Yellow Polarized Glasses	1.1	$90	http://www.smithoptics.com/Undertow_88_185.html weight includes soft sock
Swarovski Compact 10x25 Binoculars	8.0	$680	http://www.swarovskioptik.at/ or get them used on eBay
Thermarest Lite Seat	3.5	$28	http://www.thermarest.com/
Winston WT 3-piece 5-wt.	2.6	$635	http://www.winstonrods.com/wt.html

9 The Big-Bag Theory

Now that you've got all the things you want to carry, you're ready to pick out a pack. Conventional wisdom says, get all that stuff and take it down to the backpacking store and stuff it into the pack you think you want. First, see if it all fits. Second, put the thing on and walk around a bit. Try going up and down some stairs.

Aarn Natural Balance Pack & Sunday Afternoon Adventure Hat at Diamond Lake, Trinity Alps Wilderness, CA.

This is some good advice, but the packs I'm going to recommend are not all available in your local store. They are returnable to the manufacturer, but it costs you postage. So some serious thought must go into your potential selection. Or you could just order them all and send back what doesn't work.

If you have a pack already, stuff all your things into it and see if it fits. Then figure out how many cubic inches and/or liters of volume you need. At this point I should give you a quick lesson in packing.

First of all, I get rid of the stuff sacks (unnecessary weight). In general keep these rules in mind. Put the heavy stuff in the middle and near your back.

Put the light bulky stuff at the bottom and on the outside away from your back. Put the medium-density stuff on top or the sides to the right and left.

That said, here's how I pack. Before starting the procedure, I separate my gear into three groups.

1. Don't need on the trail today for sure
2. Might need on the trail today
3. Very likely will be needed on the trail today

If I'm positive it's not going to rain, I put my rain pants in the very bottom along with my book. Then I stuff in my sleeping bag and under quilt. Then all the small things, like socks, long underwear, bug head net, gloves, tank top, etc. get crammed in around the sleeping bag as tightly as possible.

From here I put in groups one and two, keeping the density rules in mind and always trying to pack tightly and compactly. Then the group three stuff goes on top and in the outside pockets. I keep my water bladder in the very top, close to my back.

When you're done the pack should be tight and compact, a streamlined unit, not lopsided, lumpy and floppy. It's best to have very few straps or items swinging around on the outside. Samwise in the *Lord of the Rings*, with his pots and pans clanking around, is not a very good backpacking role model. This stuff just gets caught on trees and bushes. Worst case scenario: you'll lose some of your gear.

So once it's all in there, you can figure out what volume pack you need. Did it barely fit? Either bring less gear or get a bigger pack. Have you got room to spare? Maybe a smaller volume pack would work.

My Favorite Packs

1. Aarn Natural Balance
2. ULA Catalyst
3. Granite Gear Vapor Trail

Let's start with the bottom of the list: the Vapor Trail. This is a classic favorite pack of through hikers and others. It's readily available so you should be able to see one locally. It's the lightest of this group at two pounds and the cheapest at about $160. I still have a couple of these and use them for day hikes. For me, the capacity at 3600 cubic inches is too small; it got me by for a couple of years though. It just took some very careful planning to pack it.

Like with sleeping bag ratings, pack capacities are not always easy to compare. I think the Vapor Trail is more like 3000 cubic inches, but it has a long extension collar that could conceivably be filled and achieve the advertised 3600 cubic inches volume. In practice this makes the pack too top heavy and the extension collar also makes access to the pack awkward. In measuring

capacity some manufactures include outside pockets, some don't. The Vapor Trail, for instance, has stretchy outside pockets that can hold quite a bit. Does the 3600 ci volume include these? I don't know.

I like a pack designed on the big-bag theory. That is, one big bag, and not a lot of pockets, zippers and compartments as these 'features' just add weight. They make it harder to fit everything where you want it. They do provide organization, but, in my opinion, at too high a price. The Vapor Trail is one big bag that loads from the top only.

So is the Catalyst. In my opinion, it's a step above the Vapor Trail in comfort. It is also bigger, heavier and more expensive. 4600 cubic inches, 2 pounds 11 ounces and $225. In this case, I think the extra weight is worth it.

Features include:
- Internal Frame Moldable to Your Back
- (4) Sizes of Pack; (5) Sizes of Hip Belt
- Dual Hip Belt Pockets
- Dry-Bag Style Top Closure

This pack is made by and for backpackers in the owner's garage in Logan, Utah. Sometimes he's out hiking for a month or more, but usually he ships pretty quickly. If you're interested in a ULA pack, call Bryan

ULA Pack in action Cuddihy Lake, Marble Mountain Wilderness, CA.

Frankle, the owner. He's a great resource, friendly and very interested in your satisfaction with his product.

I seldom fill this pack to capacity. It is built to handle a bear canister laying on it's side in the top third of the sack. Because of this the top is extra big, so I cinch it down before loading to make the top third even with the bottom two-thirds. With this adjustment the pack rides comfortably on my back. I think it's the best of the traditional internal-frame packs. And it comes in smaller, lighter, cheaper sizes as well for those who don't need so much capacity.

My favorite and current go-to pack is the Aarn Natural Balance. This New Zealand-made pack is the heaviest and most expensive of the group at four pounds seven ounces, 4600 cubic inches, $365 including shipping from New Zealand. It's the only pack of the bunch that isn't a Big Bag, it has compartments. This pack is a departure from my "light is right" philosophy.

But, it is an engineering marvel, and may well be the future of backpacking. The main innovation is the front packs. On each shoulder strap is a five-liter Balance Pocket. These front packs attach to the front hip belt with an adjustable aluminum stay that transfers the weight to your hips. The result is the front weight off-sets the back weight and the hiker, that's you, walks in an upright position; the same position you walk in everyday.

It frees your arms, shoulders and chest from constraint. The pack rides loosely on your upper body. Breathing is unrestricted. The weight is evenly distributed around your hips. There is no pressure around your shoulders that cuts off arm circulation. The pack comes in two pack sizes and two sizes of hip belt. Each size has an adjustable back length, custom moldable aluminum stays and a hip belt that can be canted to match your body. It's the most customizable of the three packs. These initial adjustments take some time, but once it's customized for your body, it's done. And it fits like a glove.

When packing this unit, you put the heavy dense items in the front packs. I pack my water bladder and food in them. They also have little pockets on the outside, great for compass, camera, glasses, all the things you want handy.

If this isn't enough, the pack itself is waterproof. It has a removable liner that I never remove except to clean it. In a conventional pack I always insert a trash compactor bag as a waterproof liner. No need with this pack. It also has a lower compartment for your sleeping bag and other lightweight compressibles. This compartment closes with a dry-bag closure and compresses the bottom nicely. Like I said, the engineering is outstanding.

This pack has pockets and features I had previously given up in favor of weight savings. The comfort factor of this pack outweighs, literally, the additional weight. But, it could be

much lighter and still retain it's fine engineering. For one thing it's made with very durable fabric. And I could do without all the pockets. So I hope Aarn makes an ultralight version of this pack soon. I think it could easily lose two pounds. Now that would be an awesome pack.

This pack can only be ordered from Aarn at this time, so you can't look it over before buying it.

Although you could probably return or exchange it (they have several models), but you'd be out the postage which is considerable. So it's a leap of faith to purchase one. The owner of this company is friendly and available by phone, so if you're interested give him a call.

The Aarn pack makes my trail time more enjoyable and safer. I'm more comfortable, balanced and stable. If you backpack often, it's worth every penny. If you backpack once a year maybe the Vapor Trail is a better choice.

One more note here. You can sell used gear on eBay. I have tried a wide variety of products. I use eBay often; both for buying and selling.

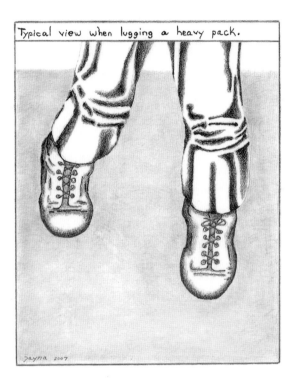

Typical view when lugging a heavy pack.

What Works For Me

Item	Oz.	Cost	Website
Aarn Natural Balance	71	$365	http://www.aarnpacks.com/products/natural_balance.html
Granite Gear Vapor Trail	32	$160	http://www.granitegear.com/products/backpacks/index.html
ULA Catalyst	43	$225	http://www.ula-equipment.com/catalyst.htm

Dogs

Dogs are a controversial subject in the wilderness. I don't want to debate that issue here. Suffice it to say, they need to be under control, not pester the wildlife or other campers. Sometimes they should just stay home.

Dog Packs

I've used a few dog packs. Some I've made myself from dry bags and harnesses. These lightweight wonders didn't last long in use. Tattered and torn, they are now in the archives, under the sewing machine.

I use a pack that provides comfort for my dogs. The harness system distributes weight evenly and comfortably. The same rules apply to packing for your dog as for packing for yourself. Heavy stuff near the body. Tight load. Nothing flapping around. And, with dogs, evenly balanced side to side.

My 50-pound dogs carry about five pounds of gear. Don't overload your dog. I have my dogs carry bulky light items, not necessarily their own gear. My vet said no packing for my dog until she was one year old. Check with your vet. Some breeds just aren't cut out for backpacking at all.

Also, like you, your dog needs to be in shape. Don't take your house-bound pet on a 50-mile, multi-day backpacking trip without any training. Take the hound with you while you train on day hikes. Have the dog wear its pack, empty at first, on short walks. Work up to load carrying.

And keep an eye on the mutt's pads. Rocky abrasive terrain, heat, cold, etc. can be hard on the paws. Snow can cling in balls to the fur around the toes. Sap and thorns can be a problem. Hydration for your dog is very important as well. You are literally your dog's keeper.

Dog Food

Kibble is super heavy, especially several day's worth. I take a freeze-dried dog food originally made for the dogs running the Iditarod. It's bio correct; I'd never heard the term either. It means it's what you might find in a wild dog's stomach. Anyway it's light, organic and made with human-grade ingredients. I guess that means you could eat it in a pinch. Never tried it though.

The dogs love it. It comes in hockey puck-like pellets that are crumbled and then re-hydrated with water. I use the bottom of the bag they come in as a dog bowl and re-package the pellets needed for a trip. I serve the dogs twelve re-hydrated medallions per day. That comes to 4-5 ounces per day per dog. Your results may vary.

My dogs with their Ruffwear Packs, Kalmiopsis Wilderness, OR.

Spoiled Dog Jammies

My dogs are short-haired Aussie mutts. Since I sleep in a hammock they aren't protected by a tent and can't do the body-heat cuddle. So jammies are my solution.

Meant for dogs in snow and freezing conditions, these coats are durable, sporting goods quality items. What can I say? I can't sleep when my dogs are shivering on the ground under me. Between these and a small ground pad the dogs are comfortable and I can rest easy.

Cocoon pullover, Thermarest Lite Seat and K9 Topcoat Body Suit, Big Duck Lake, Russian Wilderness, CA.

What Works For Me

Item	Oz.	Cost	Website
Gossamer Gear ThinLight 1/8" Pad	2.0	$9	http://www.gossamergear.com/
Homemade Sleeping Bag	18.0	NA	I used an old down sleeping bag cut to size. I replaced the zipper with hook and loop closures.
K9 Top Coat Artic Fleece Body Suit	12.8	$66	http://www.k9topcoat.com/product.asp?specific=103
Leash	0.5	free	I got a very light one free from my vet. They have them handy for wayward dogs and forgetful owners.
Nature's Variety Freeze Dried Raw 12 oz.	NA	$24	http://www.naturesvariety.com/
Ruffwear Approach Pack II large	22.2	$60	http://www.ruffwear.com/Products
Uhlr Dog Sleeping Bag	32.0	$36	http://www.uhlrgear.com/Products.htm

II The Boomer Bottom Line

If you want to skip all the explanations and reasons for gear selection and hit the ground running (well, walking comfortably anyway), then just read this chapter and call it good.

Clark Jungle Hammock Ultralight with JRB No Sniveller at Big Duck Lake, Russian Wilderness, CA.

Spend about a grand and buy the following gear items:

1. Aarn Natural Balance Pack
2. Clark Jungle Hammock (either Ultralight if you are under 5'10" or North American if you're over 5'10")
3. Jacks R Better No Sniveler Under Quilt (you gotta love that name)
4. REI Peak UL Airshock Hiking Sticks

These are all items with design features that will make your aging body happier in the back country. You'll need a sleeping bag of some sort to act as a quilt in your hammock, but you probably already have something that will do. If not, take a look at the top quilts on the Jacks R Better website or look at my sleeping-bag recommendations.

With these basics, you can pack up and forge ahead into the wild. Slowly replace your other gear. New things come out all the time.

String your hammock up in the back yard, between trees or fence posts. Spend the night out there. The colder, the better. Rain is good too. Try different hangs: tight, loose, low, high. Try pillows and stuff sacks under your knees and head. Try reading with your headlamp. Try anything that might save weight and increase comfort.

I've tested many a crazy idea in my back yard. It's nice to find out at home what doesn't really work and what does. Come up with a bad idea, and you can just walk through the back door and crawl into your civilized bed. Come up with a good idea and improve your future wilderness experiences. Then patent it and get rich. (So far this has not worked for me.)

Appendix A

This is what I generally take on a summer trip. It is my list of the primo, cost is not an issue, best of the best. See individual chapters for some cheaper options.

Appendix A: What Works For Me – Totally

Item	Oz.	Cost	Website
Aarn Natural Balance	71.0	$365	http://www.aarnpacks.com/products/natural_balance.html
ACR 0.2 oz Emergency Whistle	0.2	$3	http://www.backpackinglight.com/
Adventure Waterproof Inkjet Paper	0.4	$20	http://shop.nationalgeographic.com/product/659/3911/190.html
AirCore PRO Guyline	1.2	$24	http://www.backpackinglight.com/ Weight for 50 feet. of line
BPL Bug Head Net	0.4	$20	http://www.backpackinglight.com/
BPL Ultralight Fishing-Rod Case	3.5	$18	http://www.backpackinglight.com/
Brunton Classic Compass	1.1	$15	http://www.brunton.com/product.php?id=116
Canon Powershot SD750	4.6	$250	http://www.usa.canon.com/
Clark Ultra Light Jungle Hammock with Fly	38.0	$179	http://www.junglehammock.com/
Clear Campaign Hat Rain Cover for Tilley	1.0	$6	http://www.mtuniforms.com/catalog/index.php?cPath=25
Cocoon UL 60 Pants	6.9	$180	http://www.backpackinglight.com/
Cocoon UL 60 Pullover	8.6	$190	http://www.backpackinglight.com/

Item	Oz.	Cost	Website
Costco Reading Glasses	0.5	?	three Pack not available online
Dahlgren Hiking Socks	3.3	$17	http://www.dahlgrenfootwear.com/hiking.shtml
Flip 'n' Focus	0.8	$15	http://www.fishermaneyewear.com/ Weight includes protective cover
Gossamer Gear ThinLight 1/8" Pad	2.0	$9	http://www.gossamergear.com/
Hand Warmer Packs	1.5	$2	http://www.warmers.com/default.aspx
Hapad Comf-Orthotic Sport Insoles w/Scaphoid Pads	2.3	$20	http://www.hapad.com/hapadonline/home.php?cat=267 & http://www.hapad.com/hapadonline/home.php?cat=280
Icebreaker Bodyfit200 Mondo Zip Long Sleeve Top	9.3	$70	http://www.icebreaker.com/
ID eVent Shortie Gaiters	2.5	$30	http://www.integraldesigns.com/
Insport 5K Shorts	2.9	$20	http://www.insport.com/products.cfm?main_id=1&sub_id=1
Jacks R Better No Sniveler Under Quilt	20.0	$250	http://www.jacksrbetter.com/
JRB 10 x 11 Cat Tarp	19.0	$120	http://www.jacksrbetter.com/
K9 Top Coat Artic Fleece Body Suit	12.8	$66	http://www.k9topcoat.com/product.asp?specific=103
Kelty Triptease Lightline	2.5	$15	http://www.campmor.com/ Weight for 50 feet of line
Light Flippers	na	na	http://www.swimoutlet.com/ I got mine at a thrift store
Litech 0.9 L Kettle	5.3	$20	http://www.primus.se/

Item	Oz.	Cost	Website
Loki Hat	2.0	$25	http://www.lokiusa.com/product_detail.php?ID=H201#
Maptech Terrain Navigator Maps	na	$100	http://www.maptech.com/land/ Cost is per state
Marmot Precip Full Zip Rain Pant	10.0	$90	http://marmot.com/
Mayfly Fresh Water Pouch Lanyard	3.0	$35	http://www.mayflyhex.com/
Merrell Moab Mid GTX XCR Hikers	31.0	$120	http://www.merrell.com/
MLD eVent Rain Mitts	0.9	$45	http://www.mountainlaureldesigns.com/shop/index.php
MSR Miniworks	16.0	$85	http://www.msrgear.com/watertreatment/miniworks.asp
MSR Packtowl UL	0.7	$10	http://www.msrgear.com/camptowels/ultralite.asp
Nature's Variety Freeze Dried Raw 12 oz.	NA	$24	http://www.naturesvariety.com/
Orvis Battenkill Bar Stock III	3.5	$120	http://www.orvis.com/
Patagonia Spraymaster Rain Jacket	10.5	$300	http://www.patagonia.com/
Payless Shoes Clogs	10.0	$15	http://payless.resultspage.com/search?w=clogs
Petzl Tikka XP Headlamp	3.4	$50	http://en.petzl.com/petzl/LampesGammes?Gamme=48
Photon X-Micro LED Light	0.3	$5	http://www.backpackinglight.com/
Platypus 1.8 L Hoser	3.5	$20	http://www.platypushydration.com/
Platypus 6 L Water Tank	3.5	$20	http://www.platypushydration.com/
Possumdown Gloves	1.3	$30	http://www.backpackinglight.com/

Item	oz.	Cost	Website
Possumdown Leather Detail Crew Neck Jumper	9.0	$190	http://www.tapestryknitwear.com/homesml.asp
Possumdown Socks	1.5	$30	http://www.backpackinglight.com/
Railriders Lattitude Shirt	9.0	$64	http://www.railriders.com/
REI Peak UL Carbon Shocklight Trekking Poles	13.5	$150	http://www.rei.com/product/750835
REI Trowel	2.0	$2	http://www.rei.com/product/407146
Ruffwear Approach Pack II large	22.2	$60	http://www.ruffwear.com/Products
SD Down Sleepies	?	$30	http://sierradesigns.com/mens.display.php?id=788
Sierra Zip Stove Titanium	9.9	$129	http://zzstove.com/mcart/
Smith Undertow Yellow Polarized Glasses	1.1	$90	http://www.smithoptics.com/Undertow_88_185.html Weight includes soft sock
Spark-Lite Firestarting Kit	0.2	$10	http://www.backpackinglight.com/
Suncloud Polarized Sunglasses	0.8	$50	http://www.suncloudsunglasses.com/AGENDA_1_13.html
Swarovski Compact 10x25 Binoculars	8.0	$680	http://www.swarovskioptik.at/ or get them used on eBay
Swiss Army Knife Classic SD	0.8	$17	http://www.swissarmy.com/
Syringe for irrigating wounds	?	free	Ask for one at your local pharmacy
Thermarest Lite Seat	3.5	$28	http://www.thermarest.com/
Tilley Hat LTM6 Airflo	4.0	$60	http://www.tilley.com/
Titanium Long Handled Spoon	0.4	$13	http://www.backpackinglight.com/

Item	Oz.	Cost	Website
Titanium Tent Stakes (6)	1.5	$24	http://www.backpackinglight.com/
Tooth Powder	na	na	Check out your local health food store or just use baking soda
Ursack Major	15.0	$65	http://www.ursack.com/ursack-catalog.htm
Western Mountaineering Flight Vest	5.5	$170	http://www.westernmountaineering.com/
Western Mountaineering Highlite Sleeping Bag	16.0	$250	http://www.westernmountaineering.com/
White Sierra Trail Convertible Pants	14.8	$35	http://www.whitesierra.com/
Winston WT 3-piece 5-weight	2.6	$635	http://www.winstonrods.com/wt.html
Wintersilks Basic Long John Crew Neck	3.7	$20	http://www.wintersilks.com/
Wintersilks Light-weight Basic Long Johns	4.3	$20	http://www.wintersilks.com/
Wintersilks Spunsilk Balaclava	1.3	$14	http://www.wintersilks.com/
Wintersilks Silk/Wool Glove Liners	0.8	$13	http://www.wintersilks.com/

Appendix B

Packing Check List

Pack at home. Pull everything out. Weigh each item and check it off your list. Then pack. Put everything in, including water. Weigh your pack and note the total weight. Try your pack on and walk up and down stairs if possible. Heavy items placed nearer your center of gravity will make a big difference in the comfort of your pack. See for yourself, try different configurations. It's much easier to do at home than on the trail. Review Chapter 9 for more packing tips.

Use this chart to track your load-lightening progress.

Appendix B: Packing Check List

Date	Destination	Days	Comments	Pack Weight

Use the charts one page 94 and 95 to make sure you have everything. And weigh everything. Copy the pages and change the list to suit your needs. Be sure to use a list though, lightweight backpackers can't afford to forget anything.

X	Food (____ Days)	Oz.
	Bear Bag	
	Almonds	
	Backpack Dinners	
	Bagels or Hard Bread	
	Cayenne	
	Coffee	
	Energy Bars	
	Instant Oatmeal	
	Instant Soy Milk	
	Stevia	
	Swiss Cheese	
	Tea	
	Trail Mix	
	Turkey Jerky	
	Walnuts	
	Cup	
	Spoon	
	Stove & Pot	
	Dog Food	
	Rum	

X	Shelter	Oz.
	Bug Head Net	
	Pad or Under Quilt	
	Sleeping Bag	
	Tarp	
	Tent or Hammock	
	Tent Stakes	

X	Safety & Hygiene	Oz.
	100 feet of nylon cord	
	Collapsible Water Tank	
	Compass	
	Disposable Adjustable Lighter	
	Eye Drops	
	Fire-Starter Kit	
	First-Aid Kit	
	Hand Warmers	
	Head Light	
	Insect Repellent	
	Lip Balm	
	Maps	
	Matches (book in mini zip-lock)	
	Meds	
	Pepper Spray	
	Pocket Knife	
	Saw	
	Small Flashlight	
	Soap	
	Spare Batteries (dated mini zip-lock)	
	Sunblock	
	Toothbrush & Baking Soda	
	Trowel & TP	
	Water Bladder	
	Water Filter - check function	

X	Items Worn or Carried	Oz.
	Bandana (my only cotton item)	
	Bra	
	Convertible Pants	
	Hiking Boots	
	Hiking Sticks	
	Long Sleeve Shirt	
	Safety Necklace (whistle, etc)	
	Socks	
	Sun Glasses	
	Sun Hat	

X	Clothing Packed	Oz.
	(1) Spare Pair Socks	
	Camp Shoes	
	Cowl or Balaclava	
	Down Booties	
	Down Vest	
	Fleece Cap	
	Gloves (maybe liners too)	
	Insulated Jacket	
	Insulated Pants	
	Long Underwear Bottoms	
	Long Underwear Top	
	Rain Jacket	
	Rain Pants	
	Running Shorts/Tank Top	
	Wind Shirt	

X	Luxury Items	Oz.
	Camera with Batteries	
	Binoculars	
	Book	
	Fins	
	Fishing Gear	
	GPS	
	Sit Pad/ Floaty	

X	Other	Oz.
	Backpack	
	Change of Clothes at Car	
	Dog Bowl	
	Dog Pack	
	Leash	
	Reading Glasses	
	Trash Compactor Bag Pack Liner	

Sunday Afternoons Adventurer Hat goes for a swim at High Lake, Russian Wilderness, CA.

WHEN LIGHT IS TOO LIGHT

"PAPER TOWEL" TYPE RAIN FABRICS <u>WILL</u> KEEP YOU DRY

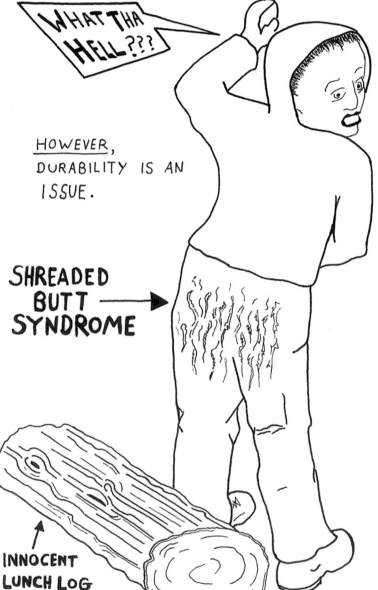

WHAT THA HELL???

HOWEVER, DURABILITY IS AN ISSUE.

SHREADED BUTT SYNDROME

INNOCENT LUNCH LOG

Appendix C

Leave-No-Trace Principles

The following is reprinted with permission from
NOLS (all rights reserved by NOLS)

Plan Ahead and Prepare

- Know the regulations and special concerns for the area you'll visit.
- Prepare for extreme weather, hazards and emergencies.
- Schedule your trip to avoid times of high use.
- Visit in small groups. Split larger parties into groups of 4-6.
- Repackage food to minimize waste.
- Use a map and compass to eliminate use of rock cairns, flagging or marking paint.

Clean water, Marble Mountains
Wilderness, CA.

Travel and Camp on Durable Surfaces

- Durable surfaces include established trails and campsites, rock, gravel, dry grasses or snow.
- Protect riparian areas by camping at least 200 feet away from lakes and streams.
- Good campsites are found, not made. Altering a site is not necessary.

In popular areas

- Walk single file in the middle of the trail, even when wet or muddy.
- Keep campsites small. Focus activity in areas where vegetation is absent.

In pristine areas

- Disperse use to prevent the creation of campsites and trails.
- Avoid places where impacts are just beginning.

Dispose of Waste Properly

- Pack it in, pack it out. Inspect your campsite and rest areas for trash or spilled foods. Pack out all trash, leftover food, and litter.
- Deposit solid human waste in cat holes dug 6 to 8 inches deep at least 200 feet from water, camp and trails. Cover and disguise the cat hole when finished.
- Pack out toilet paper and hygiene products.

- To wash yourself or your dishes, carry water 200 feet away from streams or lakes and use small amounts of biodegradable soap. Scatter strained dishwater.

Leave What you Find

- Preserve the past, observe but do not touch, cultural or historic structures and artifacts.
- Leave rocks, plants and other natural objects as you find them.

- Avoid introducing or transporting non-native species.
- Do not build structures, furniture, or dig trenches.

Minimize Campfire Impacts

- Campfires can cause lasting impacts to the backcountry. Use a lightweight stove for cooking and enjoy a candle lantern for light.
- Where fires are permitted, use established fire rings, fire pans or mound fires.
- Keep fires small. Only use sticks from the ground that can be broken by hand.
- Burn all wood and coals to ash, put out campfires completely, then scatter cool ashes.

Respect Wildlife

- Observe wildlife from a distance. Do not follow or approach them.
- Never feed animals. Feeding wildlife damages their health, alters natural behaviors, and exposes them to predators and other dangers.
- Protect wildlife and your food by storing rations and trash securely.
- Control pets at all times, or leave them at home.
- Avoid wildlife during sensitive times, mating, nesting, raising young, or winter.

Be Considerate of Other Visitors

- Respect other visitors and protect the quality of their experience.
- Be courteous, yield to other users on the trail.
- Step to the downhill side of the trail when encountering pack stock.
- Take breaks and camp away from trails and other visitors.
- Let nature's sounds prevail. Avoid loud voices and noises.

Buck Lake, Trinity Alps Wilderness, CA.

Bibliography

Highly Recommended Reading

Jardine, Ray, **Beyond Backpacking: Ray Jardine's Guide to Lightweight Hiking**, Adventurelore Press, Box 2153, Arizona City, AZ 85223, 2002, 504 pages. This book will give you a good understanding of the light-is-right philosophy. Ray has some really good ideas.

Lundin, Cody, **98.6 Degrees: The Art of Keeping Your Ass Alive**, Gibbs Smith, Publisher, PO Box 667, Layton, Utah 84041, 2003, 192 pages.
Very good information on wilderness survival for the average hiker. No chapters on how to whittle a canoe, for instance. Just reading this will make you safer in the woods.

Other Recommended Reading

Alcorn, Susan, **We're in the Mountains, Not Over the Hill**, Shepard Canyon Books, 25 Southwood Court, Oakland, CA 94611, 2003, 258 pages

Berger, Karen, **Backpacker Hiking Light Handbook,** The Mountaineers Books, 1001 SW Klickitat Way, Suite 201, Seattle, WA 98134, 2004, 171 pages

Fletcher, Colin and Chip Rawlins, **The Complete Walker IV**, Alfred A. Knopf, a division of Random House Inc., New York, 2002, revised edition, 864 pages

Jardine, Ray, **The Ray-Way Tarp Book,** Adventurelore Press, Box 2153, Arizona City, AZ 85223, 2003, 190 pages

Kestenbaum, Ryel, **The Ultralight Backpacker,** Ragged Mountain Press/McGraw-Hill, PO Box 220, Camden, ME 04843, 2001, 139 pages

Ladigin, Don, **Lighten Up! A Complete Handbook for Light and Ultralight Backpacking**, The Globe Pequot Press, PO Box 480, Guilford, Connecticut 06437, 2005, 112 pages

O'Bannon, Allen, **Allen & Mike's Really Cool Backpackin' Book**, The Globe Pequot Press, PO Box 480, Guilford, Connecticut 06437, 2001, 161 pages

Solnit, Rebecca, **Wanderlust: A History of Walking**, Penguin Putnam Inc, 375 Hudson Street, New York, New York 10014, 2001, 336 pages

Light pack = upright walking posture = great view of scenery.

Townsend, Chris, *The Advanced Backpacker: A Handbook for Year-Round, Long-Distance Hiking,* Ragged Mountain Press/McGraw-Hill, PO Box 220, Camden, ME 04843, 2001, 262 pages

Wallace, David Rains, *The Klamath Knot,* University of California Press, Berkley, CA 94720, 2003, 156 pages

Other Recommended Resources

http://www.backpackinglight.com
A great wealth of information.

http://www.backpackgeartest.org/reviews/
Independent testing by regular people.

http://bikerdave.murioi.com/
Lots of information.

http://www.hikelight.com/
Gear site.

http://www.tothewoods.net/JeffsHikingPage.html
Hammock stuff.

Lake Anna, Trinity Alps Wilderness, CA.

Photography *(all rights reserved)*

Jayna Harrison: pages 4, 5, *17, 38, 46, 49, 74*
Kathryn Reynolds: page *57*
Lara Mendel: page *40*
All other photographs by Carol Corbridge

Illustrations *(all rights reserved)*

All original art by Jayna Harrison

Receive a *FREE* sample copy of *Flyfishing & Tying Journal*!

Send an E-mail to:

CustomerService@AmatoBooks.com

or Call: **1-800-541-9498** between 8 a.m. and 5 p.m.
Monday thru Friday, or leave a message